Suite on *Spiritus Silvestre*: for Symphony

Suite on *Spiritus Silvestre*

For Symphony

Denzil Ford

dead letter office

BABEL Working Group

punctum books ✶ brooklyn, ny

SUITE ON *SPIRITUS SILVESTRE*: FOR SYMPHONY
© Denzil Ford, 2012.

First published in 2012 by
Dead Letter Office, BABEL Working Group
an imprint of punctum books
Brooklyn, New York
http://punctumbooks.com

The **BABEL Working Group** is a collective and desiring-assemblage of scholar-gypsies with no leaders or followers, no top and no bottom, and only a middle. BABEL roams and stalks the ruins of the post-historical university as a multiplicity, a pack, looking for other roaming packs and multiplicities with which to cohabit and build temporary shelters for intellectual vagabonds. We also take in strays.

ISBN-13: 978-0615747101
ISBN-10: 0615747108

Library of Congress Cataloging-in-Publication Data is available from the Library of Congress.

Table of Contents

Prelude	1
Intermezzo	5
Overture	6
Cavatina	12
There's a Hole in the Glass Flask	13
New Ways to Play an Analyzer	16
The Image King	19
Coda	21
Index of Musical Terms	23
Working Bibliography	27

▌▌▌ Suite on *Spiritus Silvestre*
For Symphony

Denzil Ford

Melody with Symphonic Accompanyment

PRELUDE[1]

Allegro grandioso

Allow me to offer the following sheet music as a movement to be played in the spirit of expressionism. Let practice of this piece become the center of transformation around which the notes and rhythms may be interpreted into a symphony in sonata form. My aim is to use the

---

[1] Please see Index of Musical terms at the end of this document.

strucutres and methods of music as a way to frame visualization of the emergence of an invisible compound in science that has come to indicate the future potential of humanity. A capella, this compound is known as carbon dioxide. We cannot see nor accurately find words for the beautiful tangle of a harmony as it vibrates in our ears, but we realize it. Nor have we seen or fully described the *spiritus silvestre* or "wild spirit"—the term used by Jan Babtist van Helmont when he first described carbon dioxide gas—that rang out as scientists characterized relationships between this gas, human behavior, and temperatures of the entire planet. By using music as a muse for thinking about carbon dioxide, new tones will be heard that remain silenced with more traditional approaches to history. This may reveal new ways outside of disciplinary boundaries to understand how objects became targets of epistemic inquiry and how they emerged as tools used for explanation or justitfication for research into new objects. Carbon dioxide will be one case study with which to explore the changes over the twentieth century in questions being asked about the atmosphere and the modifications of work structures in laboratories. Through this type of study focused on scientific objects, we will see how, along with proving global warming, the move from handmade measuring devices to commercially constructed high-precision devices changed practices in laboratories.

fff

This requires the assumption that carbon dioxide is not a single object made up of one carbon atom covalently bonded to two oxygen atoms that can change form between liquid, solid, and gas. Music is not a conglomeration of black notes on white paper. Carbon dioxide is not a compound in the atmosphere, ocean, and earth's crust that human technology tapped into and released. Rather, as a musical composition this entity is a polyphony, a suite that does real work and in most cases it does different work for different people. While it combines a number of individual but harmonizing melodies it loosely collects instrumental compositions. That is, carbon dioxide is not a static thing that was discovered—it is a multiplicity much like a piece of music. My aim is to unveil details of its movement and emergence by focusing on the practices of the scientists who made carbon dioxide come to salience. Over the course of the twentieth century, its meaning transformed from simply a component of reality into a scientific object capable of limiting human quality of life. The following arrangement provides an overview of my ideas for examining carbon dioxide as

Charles Keeling helped confirm that humans were emitting unprecedented amounts of this gas. Keeling began monitoring atmospheric carbon dioxide in the 1950s using a homemade manometer but was able to use funding from the International Geophysical Year to purchase high precision gas analyzers. I want to uncover the ways that playing these instruments created a moving—both physical and emotional—concerto that we more familiarly refer to as climatology. The Keeling curve will be treated as a type of musical score whose live production in scientific and governmental concert halls pushed carbon dioxide in the atmosphere to become more than the sum of notes written on a staff, more than numbers written on a graph.

III INTERMEZZO

III OVERTURE[2]

Capriccio

Charles Keeling's parents expected him to become a professional musician. He took formal piano lessons and played professionally for women's clubs in Chicago throughout his childhood. Although he continued to play music, Keeling's interests in the Earth, physics, and science took primacy in his career as an adult. Rather than with a musical instrument, Keeling decided to engender vibrations by measuring the physical properties of the Earth with scientific instruments. He loved being outdoors and decided to make his own instruments to measure the conditions of the "real environment."[3] Thus, he was able to make

---

[2] The preliminary details of Keeling's methods throughout the "Overture" section are from Charles D. Keeling, "Rewards and Penalties of Monitoring the Earth," *Annual Review of Energy and Environment* 23 (1998): 25–82.

[3] Keeling, "Rewards and Penalties," 32.

compelling arguments that he needed to spend copious amounts of time in nature instead of an indoor laboratory.

A chemistry professor, Harrison Brown, suggested that Keeling combine his training in chemistry with his inherent interests in geology. This was the beginning of his investigations on carbon dioxide. His first task was to build a device that would equilibrate water with a closed air supply. Keeling started with a simple hand-operated piston pump that he purchased or found laying around the laboratory. Either way, it was a device he did not design nor make. He used the pump to spray water into a closed glass chamber, which created an equilibrium between the carbon dioxide dissolved in the water and that in the air of the closed glass chamber. He referred to this device as an equilibrator. Then, he added his own version of a vacuum extraction system to isolate the carbon dioxide from the air. In a journal article from 1916 he found a reference to a design for a gas manometer that would actually measure the carbon dioxide. He then separately constructed the instrument from drawings, adding his own modifications. The equilibrator, vacuum extraction system, and gas manometer combination allowed him to collect his first sequence of air samples and measure atmospheric carbon dioxide. This work was done on the roof of the geology building at Caltech in Pasadena, California. His results from each sample varied considerably, which he attributed to the carbon dioxide emmissions from industry and cars in the area. Therefore, he moved his collection site to Big Sur State Park where he could begin to carve out a career for himself while sleeping under the stars.

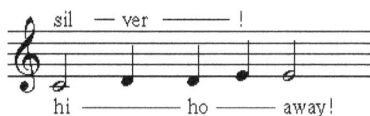

During World War II, several companies developed high precision gas analyzers that took automatic measurments of carbon dioxide concentrations in the air. These instruments came to Keeling's attention, and when the International Geophysical Year (IGY) provided the funding, he began advocating for con-tinuous monitoring of atmospheric carbon dioxide at different sites around the world.[4] IGY

---

[4] The details of Keeling's involvement with the IGY are complex and not fully fleshed out here. The continuous monitoring program took place amidst military patronage, negotiations between science and politics, and the Cold War in large part through

funding purchased four gas analyzers that were placed in different spots: Little America Station in Antarctica, Mauna Loa Observatory in Hawaii, onboard a ship, and in an indoor laboratory to provide cross-calibration. Particularly through the measurements taken at Mauna Loa, Keeling began to notice seasonal variations in carbon dioxide concentrations. By the 1960s Keeling interpreted an upward trend in carbon dioxde concentrations superimposed on the seasonal variation. He was not able to see carbon dioxide with his eyes, yet he was able to "determine" seasonal variation and an overall upward trend in concentration. Keeling accomplished this through instruments, some handmade, some commercially produced. Conceptions of carbon dioxide became a center

the Scripps Institution of Oceanography. The context in which he worked can be explored in Jacob Darwin Hamblin, *Oceanographhers and the Cold War: Disciples of Marine Science* (Seattle: University of Washington Press, 2005); Ronald Rainger, "Patronage and Science: Roger Revelle, The Navy, and Oceanography at the Scripps Institution," *Earth Sciences History: Journal of the Earth Sciences Society* 19.1 (2000): 58–89; and Elena Aronova, Karen S. Baker, and Naomi Oreskes, "Big Science and Big Data in Biology: From the International Geophysical Year through the International Biological Program to the Long Term Ecological Research (LTER) Network, 1957-Present," *Historical Studies in the Natural Sciences* 40.2 (Spring 2010): 183–224.

around which meanings concretized. The ocean-atmosphere system became *known* through the movement of carbon dioxide. The material nature of this object affected what the ocean-atmosphere system, and eventually the theory of global warming, could mean. Carbon dioxide came to be an integral component of explaining human effects on the planet as Keeling and others fused its material make-up and cultural meaning. How did carbon dioxide in the atmosphere take form as Keeling constructed detection instruments himself and used them to create knowledge? Then, how did conceptions change with commercial instruments placed around the globe? This investigation will need to take a political turn in order to determine how Keeling used the knowledge he created in his relationships between other people and groups. This proposal is limited to the work of Charles Keeling, but be certain that this line of research can be extended to many other scientists, groups, and institutions that used the instruments they made to create conceptions of global warming. In sonata form, this will not be a biography of Keeling. However, one approach might thread Keeling throughout a much larger narrative of people and institutions in a similar fashion as Emily Thompson presents Wallace Sabine in *The Soundscape of Modernity*.[5] The Keeling curve

---

[5] Emily Thompson, *The Soundscape of Modernity*

has become Keeling's opus, perhaps a more important aspect of his argument than any of his other scientific contributions. This image is now an icon of the issues surrounding climate change. To understand the power it holds, we must ask, in what ways did this image play a mediatory role between science and its cultural context? More basically, how was this image produced and disseminated, and by whom? The following movement discusses some ways that we might begin to gain a deeper understanding of what researchers on carbon dioxide were up to and how they made an abstract object not sensable without instruments into an iconic representation of reality.

(Cambridge, Mass.: MIT Press, 2004).

▌▌▌ CAVATINA

The fair breeze blew, the white foam flew,
The furrows followed free;
We were the first that ever burst
Into that silent sea.[6]

---

[6] Excerpt from Samuel Taylor Coleridge, *Annotated Ancient Mariner: The Rime of the Ancient Mariner*, (New York: Prometheus Books, 2003), 75. This poem might feed creative thinking about Keeling and his work: a long journey, ocean and air, triumph, religious references, song, spirits, and more.

▌▌▌ THERE'S A HOLE IN THE GLASS FLASK[7]

Legato

Dare to play this song: "material products of science and technology consitute knowledge," where knowledge is not reserved for the mind. Keeling learned about carbon dioxide by interacting with the world, with the instruments he built. To unravel the material culture that gave rise to carbon dioxide, we must first understand the epistemological significance of the instruments built and used. For Keeling, his combination of the equilibrator, vacuum extraction system, and gas manometer were instruments of measurement. What effect did the physical materials have on the way Keeling redesigned these instruments and the ways he interpreted their

---

[7] This section was inspired by notes from Davis Baird, *Thing Knowledge: A Philosophy of Scientific Instruments* (Berkeley: University of California Press, 2004)

interactions with his conceptions of carbon dioxide gas? How did Keeling's instruments and resultant knowledge fit into larger trends in science that relied on instruments to develop science and technology over the middle of the twentieth century? I will look for the answers in several places. Most obviously, but not to be underestimated, will be a chromatic journey through secondary literature on the history and philosophy of laboratories, objects, and mid-twentieth century political relationships. For instance:

Landscapes and Labscapes composed by Robert Kohler

Thing Knowledge composed by Davis Baird

Things That Talk composed by Lorraine Daston[8]

---

[8] Please see Working Bibliography at the end of the book for fuller citations of all three works.

My chorale must then incorporate various documents from the Keeling papers held at the Scripps Institution of Oceanography Archive. The goal in studying these documents is to look for how Keeling viewed his instruments and measurements of carbon dioxide. Additionally, I aim to find more detailed information on how he built them and conceptualized the melding of commercial made scientific instruments with his own designs and his copies of other designs. Was Keeling performing a kind of instrumental architecture? Also, I will need to look for any sort of controversy within the scientific community regarding carbon dioxide measure-ment techniques. Did everyone trust Keeling that his handmade instruments that trapped gas in flasks did exactly what he said they did? This beginning will prove fruitful in further developing an analysis of the practices carried out to measure carbon dioxide. Before any of this historical research will nestle into the corners of our brains, we must understand the way scientists visualize carbon dioxide meas-uring devices.

▮▮▮   NEW WAYS TO PLAY AN ANALYZER

Pizzicato

In order to pick apart the practices involving the high-precision gas analyzers, I propose that I visit laboratories. In these spaces I will discuss with scientists the past and present functionality of these instruments and laboratory arrangements. The Mauna Loa Observatory and the field station in Antarctica will be proper for beginning. The analyzers are still being used today to collect data on carbon dioxide concentrations. Visiting these sites and seeing first-hand how the instruments work must be combined with specific investigation into the Keeling papers. That is not to say that my experiences in these laboratories will be the same as Keeling's. Rather, to take the material nature of carbon dioxide seriously, I must also take the material nature of the instruments used to detect it seriously. Therefore, seeing, touching, and talking with scientists that use these instruments will become an integral part of my understanding of carbon dioxide's material culture. Keeling reflected upon the circumstances of using the commercial gas analyzers:

Solo, performed by Charles Keeling, 1998:

These devices detected infared radiation from a glowing coil of wire after the radiation passed through a cell in which a stream of air flowed. A radiation detector at the other end of the cell determined how much CO_2 was in the air stream. Perhaps several of these infared gas analyzers could be placed strategically around the world. I propose that my new manometric technique could be used to calibrate them precisely. Also, samples of air could be collected in 5-liter glass flasks at additional locations and returned to a laboratory to be measured by one of these instruments. Flask samples would furthermore provide much wider coverage, since continuous gas analyzers would be difficult and expensive to operate at more than a few remote locations.[9]

What exactly was done with these gas analyzers once they were placed in their field positions at Mauna Loa and Antarctica? Who kept them running? What sorts of maintenance was required? How were field assistants instructed?

---

[9] Keeling, "Rewards and Penalties," 36.

Why did scientists believe that this machine produced accurate measurements of carbon dioxide?

III THE IMAGE KING

Expressivo

Charles Keeling and The Keeling Curve, 1996[10]

The Keeling curve is an external representation of Charles Keeling's interpretation of his measurements with instruments designed to detect carbon dioxide in the atmosphere. That is, the curve is external to carbon dioxide's existence, and it is external to its interactions with the earth's ocean-atmosphere system.

---

[10] Photo courtesy of Scripps Institution of Ocean-ography Archives, UC San Diego Library (online still image collection), Digital Object URL: https://libraries.ucsd.edu/ark:/20775/bb6656382b.

Keeling's tenacity to continue carbon dioxide meaurements over the life of his career resulted in this graph that shows rising concentrations in the atmosphere from 1957 to the present. Scientists value the continuous data Keeling collected and continued carbon dioxide measurements after his death. The resultant graph plots time on the x-axis and CO_2 concentration on the y-axis. From 1957 to the present day, concentrations have risen. But I would like to investigate what exactly about this curve moved science and how was that movement related to the instruments through which scientists detect this elusive gas, this wild spirit.

⚎ CODA

Grandioso

Music is a lobster, an egg I want to use to reach new heights with the history of scientific objects and material culture.[11] Scientists do not just exchange speech and writing. They use, rearrange, swap, convert, and buy and sell physical objects in the process of measuring our world and reaching conclusions about the nature of reality. I wish to continue a recent trend in the history of science that begins to address these elements of scientific inquiry. This work holds the potential to illuminate the ways in which certain things in our world become objects of scientific inquiry and others do not. Scientific objects are not idle. Hans-Jörg

---

[11] Gilles Deleuze and Félix Guattari, *A Thousand Plateaus: Capitalism and Schizophrenia*, trans. Brian Massumi (Minneapolis: University of Minnesota Press, 1987), 39–74 and 149–66.

Rheinberger muses that, "The study of scientific objects within their experimental systems should convince us that these systems are machines for making the future."[12] In the case of carbon dioxide, the compound might actually become a machine for making the future if it has not become one already. Its increasing presence in the atmosphere in some ways is currently accepted as a determinant of the future of humanity.

> Even if they do not literally whisper and shout, these things [that talk] press their messages on attentive auditors—many messages, delicately adjusted to context, revelatory, and right on target.[13]

And sometimes, all of the talk and chatter morphs into a cadence utilizing rhythms & tones and notes & beats that allow these things to convey their messages with a sense of musicality.

---

[12] Lorraine Daston, ed., *Biographies of Objects* (Chicago: University of Chicago Press, 2000), 294.

[13] Lorraine Daston, *Things That Talk: Object Lessons From Art and Science* (New York: Zone Books, 2004), 12.

Clef

In sheet music, a symbol at the beginning of the staff defining the pitch of the notes found in that particular staff.

Fortissimo

A direction to play very loud.

Breath mark

A direction for a general pause.

A capella

One or more vocalists performing without accompaniment.

Allegro

A direction to play lively and fast.

Capriccio

A quick, improvisational, spirited piece of music.

Chorale　　　　Hymn sung by the choir and congregation in unison.

Chromoatic　　Referring to a scale that includes all twelve notes of an octave and so makes progression in semitones.

Concerto　　　A composition written for a solo instrument. The soloist plays the melody while the orchestra plays the accompaniment.

Expressionism　Atonal style used as a means of evoking heightened emotions and states of mind.

Grandioso　　　Word to indicate that the movement or entire composition is to be played grandly.

Intermezzo　　Short movement or interlude connecting the main parts of the composition.

Legato　　　　Word to indicate that the movement or entire composition is to be played smoothly.

Movement   A separate section of a larger composition.

Overture   Introduction to an opera or other large musical work.

Polyphony   Combining a number of individual but harmonizing melodies.

Prelude   A short piece introducing what is to come.

Rhythm   The element of music pertaining to time, played as a grouping of notes into accented and unaccented beats.

Score   Handwritten sheet music.

Staff   Made up of five horizontal parallel lines and the spaces between them on which musical notation is written.

Suite   A loose collection of instrumental compositions.

Tone   The intonation, pitch, and

modulation of a composition expressing the meaning, feeling, or attitude of the music.

▌▌▌ WORKING BIBLIOGRAPHY

GLOBAL WARMING AND CLIMATE CHANGE

Charney, Jule G. *On the Scale of Atmospheric Motions*. Oslo: Grodahl & Sons, 1948.

Charney, Jule G. and J. Shukla. *Dynamics of Large-Scale Atmospheric and Oceanic Processes: Selected Papers of Jule Gregory Charney*. Hampton: A. Deepak Publishing, 2001.

Crawford, Elisabeth T. *Arrhenius: From Ionic Theory to the Greenhouse Effect*. Sagamore Beach: Science History Publications/USA, 1996.

de Steiguer, Joseph E. *The Origins of Modern Environmental Thought*. Tucson: University of Arizona Press, 2006.

Ehleringer, James R., Thure E. Cerling, and M. Denise Dearing. *A History of Atmospheric CO_2 and Its Effects on Plants, Animals, and Ecosystems*. New York: Springer, 2005.

Fleming, James R. *Historical Perspectives on Climate Change*. Oxford: Oxford University Press, 1998.

Fleming, James R. *Meteorology in America, 1800-1870*. Baltimore: Johns Hopkins University Press, 1990.

Fleming, James R. *The Callendar Effect: The Life and Times of Guy Stewart Callendar (1898-1964)*. Boston: American Meteorological Society, 2007.

Fleming, James R., Vladimir Jankovic, and Deborah R. Coen. *Intimate Universality: Local and Global Themes in the History of Weather and Climate*. Sagamore Beach: Science History Publication/USA, 2006.

Fleming, James R., and Henry A. Gemery. *Science, Technology, and the Environment*. Akron: University of Akron Press, 1994.

Gruber, Nicolas, and Charles D. Keeling. *Seasonal Carbon Cycling in the Sargasso Sea Near Bermuda*. Berkeley: University of California Press, 1999.

Guenther, Peter, R., Charles D. Keeling, and Guy Emanuele. *Oceanic CO_2 Measurements for the WOCE Hydrographic Survey in the Pacific Ocean, 1990-1991: Shore Based*

Analysis. San Diego: Scripps Institution of Oceanography, 1994.

Heimann, Martin, and Charles D. Keeling. *A Three-Dimensional Model of Atmospheric CO_2 Transport Based on Observed Winds: Model Description and Stimulated Tracer Experiments*. Hamburg: Max Planck Institute for Meteorology, 1989.

Weart, Spencer. *The Discovery of Global Warming*. Cambridge, Mass.: Harvard University Press, 2003.

Weart, Spencer. *The Discover of Global Warming: A Hypertext History of How Scientists Came to (partly) Understand What People Are Doing to Cause Climate Change* [website]. 2003-2011: http://www.aip.org/history/climate.

White, Robert. "Whither the U.S. climate program? (Environment & Energy)." *Issues in Science and Technology* 19.4 (2003): 51.

INSTRUMENTS AND OBJECTS

Baird, Davis. *Thing Knowledge: A Philosophy of Scientific Instruments*. Berkeley: University of California Press, 2004.

Daston, Lorraine. *Things That Talk: Object Lessons From Art and Science.* New York: Zone Books, 2004.

Galison, Peter, ed. *The Architecture of Science.* Cambridge, Mass.: MIT Press, 1999.

Jaffe, Herbert. *The Construction of an Improved Mercury Manometer and the Meniscus Correction.* B.S. Thesis, Massachusetts Institute of Technology, Dept. of General Science, 1939.

Jones, Barry E. *Instrument Science and Technology.* Bristol: A. Hilger, 1982.

Kohler, Robert E. *Landscapes and Labscapes: Exploring the Lab-Field Border in Biology.* Chicago: University of Chicago Press, 2002.

Prowse, David B. *The Effect of Mercury-Vapour Pressure in a Mercury Manometer.* Ascot Vale: Materials Research Laboratories, 1978.

LABORATORY AND PRACTICE

Feest, Uljana, Giora Hon, Hans-Jörg Rheinberger, Jutta Schickore, and Fredrich Steinle, eds. *Generating Experiemental Knowledge.* Berlin: Max Planck Institute for the History of Science, 2008.

Kuklick, Henrika and Robert E. Kohler. *Science in the Field*. Chicago: University of Chicago Press, 1996.

Hacking, Ian. *Representing and Intervening*. Cambridge, Eng.: Cambridge University Press, 1983.

Keeling, Charles, D. *Instructions for Taking Air Samples on Board Ship: Carbon Dioxide Project*. La Jolla: Institute of Marine Resources, 1971.

MUSIC AND MUSING

De Landa, Mauel. *A Thousand Years of Nonlinear History*. New York: Zone Books, 1997.

Deleuze, Gilles and Félix Guattari. *A Thousand Plateaus: Capitalism and Schizophrenia*. Minneapolis: University of Minnesota Press, 1987.

Dowd, Timothy, J. *The Sociology of Music: Sounds, songs, and society*. Thousand Oaks, Calif.: Sage, 2005.

Dunaway, Finis. "Seeing Global Warming: Contemporary Art and the Fate of the Planet." *Environmental History* 14.1 (2009): 9–31.

Gozza, Paola. *Number to Sound: The Musical Way to the Scientific Revolution.* Boston: Kluwer Academic Publishers, 2000.

Thompson, Emily. *The Soundscapes of Modernity: Architectural Acoustics and the Culture of Listening in America, 1900-1933.* Cambridge, Mass.: MIT Press, 2002.

W. dreams, like Phaedrus, of an army of thinker-friends, thinker-lovers. He dreams of a thought-army, a thought-pack, which would storm the philosophical Houses of Parliament. He dreams of Tartars from the philosophical steppes, of thought-barbarians, thought-outsiders. What distances would shine in their eyes!

~Lars Iyer

www.babelworkinggroup.org

Charles Keeling playing the piano in his home
(1984); photo courtesy of Scripps Institution of
Oceanography Archives, UC San Diego Library,
(online still image collection), Digital Object URL:
https://libraries.ucsd.edu/ark:/20775/ bb5427841d.